50 Flavors of Africa Recipes

By: Kelly Johnson

Table of Contents

- Jollof Rice (Nigeria)
- Bunny Chow (South Africa)
- Ugali with Sukuma (Kenya)
- Ethiopian Doro Wat
- Biltong (South Africa)
- Moroccan Tagine
- Piri Piri Chicken (Mozambique)
- Mafé (Senegal)
- Fufu with Groundnut Soup (Ghana)
- Nyama Choma (Kenya)
- Boerewors (South Africa)
- Injera with Tibs (Ethiopia)
- Cape Malay Curry (South Africa)
- West African Pepper Soup
- Maize Porridge (Kenya)
- Moroccan Couscous
- Nigerian Moi Moi
- Seychelles Fish Curry
- Tanzanian Mandazi
- Ghanaian Kelewele
- Algerian Couscous with Lamb
- Egyptian Koshari
- Malagasy Chicken (Madagascar)
- Sudanese Kisra
- Zanzibar Pilaf (Tanzania)
- Egyptian Fatta
- Ethiopian Shiro
- Nigerian Pepper Chicken
- Moroccan Mechoui
- South African Malva Pudding
- Nigerian Akara
- Egyptian Mahshi
- Somali Samosas
- Ghanaian Jollof Rice
- Liberian Palava Sauce

- Nigerian Efo Riro
- South African Chakalaka
- Tunisian Brik
- Senegalese Thieboudienne
- Ugandan Rolex
- Malawian Nsima with Stew
- Moroccan Harira Soup
- Nigerian Ofada Rice with Ayamase
- Kenyan Samosa
- West African Groundnut Stew
- Sudanese Ful Medames
- Somali Camel Stew
- Namibian Potjie
- Tanzanian Sukuma with Eggs
- Ivory Coast Attiéké with Fish

Jollof Rice (Nigeria)

Ingredients:

- 2 cups long-grain rice
- 1/4 cup vegetable oil
- 1 onion, chopped
- 2 tomatoes, chopped
- 1 red bell pepper
- 1 tbsp tomato paste
- 2 cups chicken broth
- 1 tsp thyme
- 1 tsp curry powder
- 1 tsp paprika
- Salt and pepper to taste
- 1/2 cup peas (optional)

Instructions:

1. Heat oil in a pot and sauté onions until translucent.
2. Blend tomatoes, bell pepper, and tomato paste. Add to onions and cook until the sauce thickens.
3. Stir in rice, then add chicken broth, thyme, curry powder, paprika, salt, and pepper.
4. Cover and cook on low heat for 25-30 minutes. Add peas in the last 5 minutes.

Bunny Chow (South Africa)

Ingredients:

- 1 loaf of white bread
- 2 cups cooked chicken or lamb, shredded
- 1 onion, chopped
- 2 tomatoes, chopped
- 1 tbsp curry powder
- 1 tsp turmeric
- 1/2 tsp cumin
- 1 tbsp vegetable oil
- 1 cup chicken broth
- Salt to taste
- Fresh cilantro for garnish

Instructions:

1. Heat oil in a pan and sauté onions until soft. Add tomatoes, curry powder, turmeric, cumin, and cook for 5 minutes.
2. Stir in the shredded chicken or lamb and chicken broth. Simmer for 10 minutes.
3. Cut a loaf of bread into halves or quarters, hollow out the center.
4. Fill the bread with the curry mixture and garnish with cilantro.

Ugali with Sukuma (Kenya)

Ingredients for Ugali:

- 2 cups maize flour (cornmeal)
- 4 cups water
- Salt to taste

Ingredients for Sukuma:

- 1 bunch sukuma (collard greens), chopped
- 1 onion, chopped
- 2 tomatoes, chopped
- 2 tbsp vegetable oil
- 1 tsp garlic, minced
- Salt and pepper to taste

Instructions for Ugali:

1. Boil water with a pinch of salt. Slowly stir in maize flour.
2. Stir continuously to prevent lumps. Cook until the mixture thickens and pulls away from the sides of the pot.

Instructions for Sukuma:

1. Heat oil in a pan, sauté onions and garlic until soft.
2. Add tomatoes and cook for 5 minutes.
3. Stir in sukuma greens, season with salt and pepper, and cook for 5-7 minutes until tender.

Ethiopian Doro Wat

Ingredients:

- 1 lb chicken drumsticks or thighs
- 2 tbsp niter kibbeh (Ethiopian spiced butter)
- 1 onion, chopped
- 2 cloves garlic, minced
- 1 tbsp ginger, grated
- 2 tbsp berbere spice mix
- 1 cup tomato paste
- 2 cups chicken broth
- 3 boiled eggs
- Salt to taste

Instructions:

1. Heat niter kibbeh in a large pot. Sauté onions, garlic, and ginger until soft.
2. Add berbere spice mix and cook for 1-2 minutes.
3. Stir in chicken and brown on all sides.
4. Add tomato paste and chicken broth, simmer for 30-40 minutes.
5. Add boiled eggs and cook for an additional 10 minutes.

Biltong (South Africa)

Ingredients:

- 1 lb beef (sirloin or rump)
- 2 tbsp brown sugar
- 1 tbsp coriander seeds
- 1 tbsp black pepper
- 1 tbsp salt
- 1/4 cup vinegar
- 1/4 cup Worcestershire sauce

Instructions:

1. Mix sugar, coriander, pepper, and salt. Rub this mixture on the beef.
2. Soak the beef in vinegar and Worcestershire sauce for 30 minutes.
3. Hang beef in a cool, dry place for 3-7 days, depending on desired dryness.

Moroccan Tagine

Ingredients:

- 1 lb chicken or lamb
- 2 tbsp olive oil
- 1 onion, chopped
- 2 garlic cloves, minced
- 1 tsp ground cumin
- 1 tsp ground coriander
- 1/2 tsp cinnamon
- 2 cups chicken broth
- 1 cup dried apricots, chopped
- 1 can chickpeas, drained
- 1/2 cup almonds, toasted
- Salt and pepper to taste

Instructions:

1. Heat oil in a tagine or pot, brown meat on all sides.
2. Add onion, garlic, and spices, cook for 5 minutes.
3. Stir in chicken broth, apricots, chickpeas, and simmer for 45 minutes.
4. Garnish with toasted almonds and serve with couscous.

Piri Piri Chicken (Mozambique)

Ingredients:

- 4 chicken thighs or breasts
- 1/4 cup piri piri sauce
- 1 tbsp garlic, minced
- 1 tbsp lemon juice
- 1 tbsp olive oil
- Salt and pepper to taste

Instructions:

1. Mix piri piri sauce, garlic, lemon juice, olive oil, salt, and pepper.
2. Marinate chicken for 1-2 hours.
3. Grill or bake chicken until cooked through, about 30 minutes.

Mafé (Senegal)

Ingredients:

- 1 lb beef, lamb, or chicken, cut into chunks
- 2 tbsp vegetable oil
- 1 onion, chopped
- 1 bell pepper, chopped
- 2 tomatoes, chopped
- 1/4 cup peanut butter
- 2 cups chicken broth
- 1 tbsp garlic, minced
- 1 tsp ground ginger
- Salt and pepper to taste

Instructions:

1. Brown meat in oil. Remove and set aside.
2. Sauté onion, bell pepper, and tomatoes.
3. Stir in peanut butter, chicken broth, garlic, and ginger.
4. Return meat to the pot, simmer for 40 minutes, season to taste.

Fufu with Groundnut Soup (Ghana)

Ingredients for Fufu:

- 2 lbs yam or cassava, peeled and chopped
- Water

Ingredients for Groundnut Soup:

- 1/2 cup peanut butter
- 1 lb chicken or beef, cut into pieces
- 1 onion, chopped
- 2 tomatoes, chopped
- 2 cups chicken broth
- 1 tbsp ginger, minced
- Salt and pepper to taste

Instructions for Fufu:

1. Boil yams or cassava until tender.
2. Mash and pound until smooth and stretchy.

Instructions for Groundnut Soup:

1. Brown meat in a pot, then set aside.
2. Sauté onions, tomatoes, and ginger. Add peanut butter and chicken broth.
3. Stir in meat and simmer for 30 minutes. Serve with fufu.

Nyama Choma (Kenya)

Ingredients:

- 2 lbs beef, goat, or chicken, cut into cubes
- 3 tbsp vegetable oil
- 2 tbsp soy sauce
- 2 tbsp lemon juice
- 1 tbsp ginger, minced
- 1 tbsp garlic, minced
- 1 tbsp paprika
- 1 tsp cumin
- 1 tsp coriander
- Salt and pepper to taste
- Skewers

Instructions:

1. Mix oil, soy sauce, lemon juice, ginger, garlic, paprika, cumin, coriander, salt, and pepper to make a marinade.
2. Marinate the meat for 2-4 hours.
3. Skewer the marinated meat and grill or roast over medium heat until cooked to your desired doneness.
4. Serve with Ugali, sukuma, or a salad.

Boerewors (South Africa)

Ingredients:

- 2 lbs beef, minced
- 1 lb pork, minced
- 1/2 cup breadcrumbs
- 2 cloves garlic, minced
- 2 tbsp coriander seeds, ground
- 1 tbsp black pepper
- 1 tsp ground cloves
- 1 tsp ground nutmeg
- 2 tbsp vinegar
- 1/4 cup water
- Sausage casings

Instructions:

1. Mix the beef, pork, garlic, spices, vinegar, and water in a large bowl.
2. Stuff the sausage mixture into casings, twisting at intervals to form links.
3. Grill the sausages over medium heat until cooked through, about 15-20 minutes.
4. Serve with pap and tomato sauce.

Injera with Tibs (Ethiopia)

Ingredients for Injera:

- 2 cups teff flour
- 3 cups water
- 1/4 tsp active dry yeast
- 1/4 tsp baking soda
- Salt to taste

Ingredients for Tibs:

- 1 lb beef or lamb, cubed
- 2 tbsp vegetable oil
- 1 onion, chopped
- 2 garlic cloves, minced
- 2 tbsp berbere spice mix
- 1 tbsp ginger, minced
- 1/2 cup chicken broth
- Salt to taste

Instructions for Injera:

1. Mix teff flour, water, and yeast. Let the batter ferment for 2-3 days.
2. Pour the batter onto a hot non-stick skillet, swirling to form a pancake-like shape. Cook until bubbles form, then remove from heat.

Instructions for Tibs:

1. Heat oil in a pan and sauté onions and garlic until soft.
2. Add meat, berbere spice mix, and ginger. Cook until the meat is browned.
3. Stir in chicken broth and cook for an additional 10 minutes.
4. Serve the tibs on top of the injera.

Cape Malay Curry (South Africa)

Ingredients:

- 1 lb chicken or lamb, cut into pieces
- 2 tbsp vegetable oil
- 1 onion, chopped
- 2 cloves garlic, minced
- 1 tbsp ginger, minced
- 2 tbsp curry powder
- 1 tbsp cinnamon
- 1 tsp turmeric
- 1 can diced tomatoes
- 1 cup coconut milk
- 1 tbsp sugar
- Salt and pepper to taste

Instructions:

1. Heat oil in a pot and sauté onions, garlic, and ginger until softened.
2. Add curry powder, cinnamon, turmeric, and cook for 2 minutes.
3. Add the meat and cook until browned.
4. Stir in tomatoes, coconut milk, sugar, salt, and pepper. Simmer for 30-40 minutes.
5. Serve with rice or flatbread.

West African Pepper Soup

Ingredients:

- 1 lb chicken, fish, or goat, cut into pieces
- 1 onion, chopped
- 2 cloves garlic, minced
- 2 tbsp ginger, minced
- 1 tbsp ground pepper
- 1 tbsp thyme
- 1 tbsp cloves
- 1-2 scotch bonnet peppers (optional)
- 4 cups water
- Salt to taste

Instructions:

1. In a pot, add the meat, onions, garlic, ginger, and spices.
2. Pour in water and bring to a boil.
3. Reduce heat and simmer for 30-40 minutes until the meat is tender.
4. Season with salt and serve hot.

Maize Porridge (Kenya)

Ingredients:

- 1 cup maize flour (cornmeal)
- 4 cups water
- 1/2 cup milk (optional)
- 1 tbsp sugar (optional)
- Pinch of salt

Instructions:

1. Boil water in a saucepan.
2. Gradually add maize flour while stirring to prevent lumps.
3. Reduce heat and cook, stirring continuously, for 15-20 minutes.
4. Add milk and sugar, if using, and cook until the porridge thickens.
5. Serve warm as a breakfast dish.

Moroccan Couscous

Ingredients:

- 2 cups couscous
- 2 cups vegetable or chicken broth
- 1 tbsp olive oil
- 1/2 tsp salt
- 1/4 tsp cumin
- 1/4 tsp cinnamon
- 1/2 cup raisins
- 1/2 cup almonds, toasted

Instructions:

1. Bring the broth to a boil and stir in couscous, olive oil, salt, cumin, and cinnamon.
2. Cover and let it steam for 5 minutes.
3. Fluff with a fork and stir in raisins and almonds.
4. Serve as a side dish or with a tagine.

Nigerian Moi Moi

Ingredients:

- 2 cups beans (black-eyed peas or brown beans), peeled
- 1 onion, chopped
- 2 tomatoes, chopped
- 2 cloves garlic, minced
- 1 tsp ginger, minced
- 1/4 cup vegetable oil
- 2 tbsp ground crayfish (optional)
- 1/2 tsp ground pepper
- 2 cups water
- Salt to taste
- Banana leaves or foil for wrapping

Instructions:

1. Blend the peeled beans with onions, tomatoes, garlic, ginger, and water.
2. Stir in the vegetable oil, crayfish, pepper, and salt.
3. Pour the mixture into banana leaves or foil.
4. Steam the wrapped mixture for 45 minutes or until set.

Seychelles Fish Curry

Ingredients:

- 1 lb fish fillets (tuna, snapper, or any firm fish)
- 2 tbsp vegetable oil
- 1 onion, chopped
- 1 tomato, chopped
- 2 cloves garlic, minced
- 1 tbsp curry powder
- 1 tsp turmeric
- 1/2 cup coconut milk
- 1 tbsp lime juice
- Salt and pepper to taste

Instructions:

1. Heat oil in a pan and sauté onions, garlic, and tomatoes until soft.
2. Add curry powder and turmeric, cook for 2 minutes.
3. Stir in fish fillets, coconut milk, and lime juice. Simmer for 10-15 minutes.
4. Season with salt and pepper. Serve with rice.

Tanzanian Mandazi

Ingredients:

- 2 cups all-purpose flour
- 1/4 cup sugar
- 1 tsp baking powder
- 1/4 tsp ground cardamom
- 1/4 cup coconut milk
- 1/4 cup water
- 1 egg
- 1 tbsp butter, melted
- Vegetable oil for frying
- Pinch of salt

Instructions:

1. In a large bowl, combine flour, sugar, baking powder, cardamom, and salt.
2. Add the egg, melted butter, coconut milk, and water, then knead into a soft dough.
3. Let the dough rest for 30 minutes.
4. Roll out the dough and cut into triangles or squares.
5. Heat oil in a pan and fry the mandazi until golden brown on both sides.
6. Drain on paper towels and serve warm.

Ghanaian Kelewele

Ingredients:

- 3 large plantains, peeled and cut into bite-sized pieces
- 1 tbsp ginger, minced
- 1 tbsp garlic, minced
- 1-2 scotch bonnet peppers, minced
- 1 tbsp ground paprika
- 1 tsp ground cayenne pepper
- 1 tbsp ground cinnamon
- 1 tsp salt
- 1 tbsp vegetable oil

Instructions:

1. In a bowl, mix ginger, garlic, scotch bonnet peppers, paprika, cayenne, cinnamon, and salt.
2. Toss the plantain pieces in the spice mixture to coat evenly.
3. Heat oil in a pan and fry the plantains until golden brown and crispy.
4. Drain on paper towels and serve hot.

Algerian Couscous with Lamb

Ingredients:

- 2 cups couscous
- 1 lb lamb, cut into chunks
- 1 onion, chopped
- 2 carrots, peeled and chopped
- 2 zucchinis, chopped
- 1 can chickpeas, drained
- 2 tomatoes, chopped
- 2 tbsp olive oil
- 1 tbsp cumin
- 1 tsp cinnamon
- 1 tsp ground ginger
- 4 cups beef broth
- Salt and pepper to taste

Instructions:

1. Heat olive oil in a large pot and brown the lamb chunks.
2. Add onions, carrots, zucchinis, tomatoes, cumin, cinnamon, ginger, and cook for 5 minutes.
3. Pour in the beef broth and bring to a boil. Simmer for 1 hour until lamb is tender.
4. Steam the couscous according to package instructions.
5. Serve the lamb stew over couscous, garnished with chickpeas.

Egyptian Koshari

Ingredients:

- 1 cup rice
- 1 cup lentils
- 1 cup elbow macaroni
- 2 onions, thinly sliced
- 2 cloves garlic, minced
- 2 tbsp vegetable oil
- 2 cups tomato sauce
- 1 tsp cumin
- 1/2 tsp chili powder
- Salt to taste
- 1 tbsp vinegar

Instructions:

1. Cook the rice, lentils, and macaroni separately, then set aside.
2. In a pan, heat oil and fry the onions until crispy, then remove and set aside.
3. In the same pan, sauté garlic, then add tomato sauce, cumin, chili powder, and vinegar. Simmer for 10 minutes.
4. Layer the rice, lentils, and macaroni on a plate, then top with the tomato sauce and crispy onions.
5. Serve hot.

Malagasy Chicken (Madagascar)

Ingredients:

- 4 chicken thighs, bone-in
- 1 onion, chopped
- 3 cloves garlic, minced
- 1 tbsp ginger, minced
- 2 tbsp vegetable oil
- 1 tbsp curry powder
- 1 can coconut milk
- 1 tbsp soy sauce
- 1/2 tsp turmeric
- 1 tbsp brown sugar
- Salt to taste

Instructions:

1. Heat oil in a pan and sauté onions, garlic, and ginger until soft.
2. Add chicken and brown on all sides.
3. Stir in curry powder, turmeric, soy sauce, and brown sugar.
4. Add coconut milk and simmer for 30 minutes until the chicken is cooked through.
5. Serve with rice.

Sudanese Kisra

Ingredients:

- 2 cups sorghum flour
- 1 cup water
- 1/2 tsp salt

Instructions:

1. Mix sorghum flour, water, and salt into a smooth batter.
2. Heat a large griddle or skillet and pour a thin layer of the batter.
3. Cook for 2-3 minutes on each side until golden brown.
4. Serve with stews or sauces.

Zanzibar Pilaf (Tanzania)

Ingredients:

- 2 cups rice
- 2 cups coconut milk
- 1 onion, chopped
- 2 cloves garlic, minced
- 1 cinnamon stick
- 1 bay leaf
- 1/2 tsp ground turmeric
- 1 tbsp vegetable oil
- Salt to taste

Instructions:

1. Heat oil in a pot and sauté onions and garlic until soft.
2. Add turmeric, cinnamon stick, bay leaf, and rice, then stir to coat.
3. Pour in the coconut milk and bring to a boil.
4. Lower the heat and simmer for 15-20 minutes, or until the rice is cooked.
5. Fluff with a fork and serve.

Egyptian Fatta

Ingredients:

- 1 lb beef or lamb, cut into pieces
- 4 cups beef broth
- 4 slices pita bread, torn into pieces
- 3 cloves garlic, minced
- 2 tbsp tomato paste
- 1 tbsp vinegar
- 1 tsp cumin
- Salt and pepper to taste

Instructions:

1. Boil the meat in beef broth for 1-2 hours until tender.
2. In a separate pan, sauté garlic in oil, then add tomato paste and cook for 5 minutes.
3. Add the vinegar, cumin, and salt to the meat broth.
4. In a serving dish, layer torn pita bread, then pour over the meat and broth.
5. Serve hot.

Ethiopian Shiro

Ingredients:

- 2 cups chickpea flour
- 1 onion, chopped
- 2 cloves garlic, minced
- 1 tbsp ginger, minced
- 1 tbsp berbere spice mix
- 1/4 cup tomato paste
- 3 cups water
- 2 tbsp vegetable oil
- Salt to taste

Instructions:

1. Heat oil in a pan and sauté onions, garlic, and ginger until soft.
2. Stir in berbere spice mix and tomato paste.
3. Gradually add chickpea flour and water, stirring constantly to avoid lumps.
4. Simmer for 15-20 minutes, then season with salt.
5. Serve with injera.

Nigerian Pepper Chicken

Ingredients:

- 4 chicken thighs, cut into pieces
- 1 onion, chopped
- 3 cloves garlic, minced
- 1 tbsp ginger, minced
- 2-3 scotch bonnet peppers, minced
- 2 tbsp vegetable oil
- 2 tbsp tomato paste
- 1 cup chicken broth
- Salt and pepper to taste

Instructions:

1. Heat oil in a pan and brown the chicken pieces.
2. Add onions, garlic, ginger, and scotch bonnet peppers, cooking until fragrant.
3. Stir in tomato paste, chicken broth, salt, and pepper.
4. Simmer for 25-30 minutes until the chicken is fully cooked.
5. Serve with rice or fried plantains.

Moroccan Mechoui

Ingredients:

- 4 lbs whole lamb shoulder or leg
- 1/4 cup olive oil
- 4 cloves garlic, minced
- 1 tbsp ground cumin
- 1 tbsp ground coriander
- 1 tbsp paprika
- 1 tsp cinnamon
- Salt and pepper to taste
- Fresh cilantro for garnish
- Lemon wedges for serving

Instructions:

1. Preheat your oven to 350°F (175°C).
2. Rub the lamb with olive oil, garlic, cumin, coriander, paprika, cinnamon, salt, and pepper.
3. Place the lamb in a roasting pan and roast for 2.5 to 3 hours, basting occasionally with its own juices.
4. Once tender, remove from the oven and let it rest for 10 minutes.
5. Shred the lamb and serve with cilantro and lemon wedges.

South African Malva Pudding

Ingredients:

- 1 cup all-purpose flour
- 1 tsp baking soda
- 1/4 tsp salt
- 1 egg
- 1/2 cup sugar
- 1 tbsp apricot jam
- 1/4 cup milk
- 1/4 cup melted butter
- 1 tbsp vinegar
- 1 tsp vanilla extract

For the sauce:

- 1/2 cup heavy cream
- 1/4 cup sugar
- 1/4 cup butter
- 1/4 cup water

Instructions:

1. Preheat your oven to 350°F (175°C). Grease a baking dish.
2. In a bowl, combine flour, baking soda, and salt. In another bowl, whisk the egg, sugar, apricot jam, milk, melted butter, vinegar, and vanilla.
3. Add the dry ingredients to the wet ingredients and mix until smooth.
4. Pour the batter into the prepared baking dish and bake for 30-35 minutes.
5. While baking, prepare the sauce by heating cream, sugar, butter, and water in a saucepan until melted.
6. Pour the hot sauce over the pudding once it's done baking. Let it soak in before serving.

Nigerian Akara

Ingredients:

- 2 cups black-eyed peas
- 1 onion, chopped
- 2 cloves garlic, minced
- 2-3 scotch bonnet peppers, minced
- 1 tsp ground ginger
- 1/2 tsp salt
- Vegetable oil for frying

Instructions:

1. Soak the black-eyed peas overnight, then peel off the skins.
2. Blend the peas, onion, garlic, scotch bonnet peppers, ginger, and salt in a food processor until smooth.
3. Heat oil in a deep pan or fryer.
4. Scoop spoonfuls of the batter and carefully drop into the hot oil. Fry until golden brown and crispy.
5. Drain on paper towels and serve hot.

Egyptian Mahshi

Ingredients:

- 4 medium zucchinis, hollowed out
- 1 cup rice
- 1/2 lb ground beef or lamb
- 1 onion, chopped
- 2 tomatoes, chopped
- 2 tbsp tomato paste
- 1/2 tsp cinnamon
- 1/2 tsp allspice
- Salt and pepper to taste
- Fresh parsley for garnish

Instructions:

1. In a pan, sauté onions and ground meat until browned.
2. Stir in rice, chopped tomatoes, tomato paste, cinnamon, allspice, salt, and pepper. Cook for 5 minutes.
3. Stuff the zucchini with the rice mixture, being careful not to overfill.
4. Arrange the stuffed zucchini in a pot, adding enough water to cover.
5. Bring to a boil, then simmer for 40-45 minutes.
6. Garnish with fresh parsley and serve.

Somali Samosas

Ingredients:

- 1 lb ground beef or lamb
- 1 onion, chopped
- 2 cloves garlic, minced
- 1 tbsp ground cumin
- 1 tsp ground coriander
- 1 tsp ground turmeric
- 1/2 tsp ground cinnamon
- 2 tbsp cilantro, chopped
- 1 package of samosa wrappers or phyllo dough
- Vegetable oil for frying
- Salt and pepper to taste

Instructions:

1. Heat a pan and cook the ground meat until browned.
2. Add onions, garlic, cumin, coriander, turmeric, cinnamon, and salt. Stir until fragrant.
3. Remove from heat and mix in cilantro.
4. Place a spoonful of the mixture onto the samosa wrappers and fold into triangles, sealing the edges with a little water.
5. Heat oil in a pan and fry the samosas until golden brown and crispy.
6. Drain on paper towels and serve with a dipping sauce.

Ghanaian Jollof Rice

Ingredients:

- 2 cups long-grain rice
- 1 onion, chopped
- 1 red bell pepper, chopped
- 2 tomatoes, blended
- 1/4 cup tomato paste
- 1 tbsp ground ginger
- 1 tbsp ground cumin
- 1 tbsp curry powder
- 2 cups chicken broth
- 1/4 cup vegetable oil
- Salt and pepper to taste

Instructions:

1. Heat oil in a pot and sauté onions and bell peppers until soft.
2. Stir in blended tomatoes, tomato paste, ginger, cumin, curry powder, salt, and pepper. Cook for 10 minutes.
3. Add rice and stir to coat in the sauce.
4. Pour in chicken broth, cover, and simmer for 20-25 minutes until the rice is cooked and the liquid is absorbed.
5. Fluff the rice and serve.

Liberian Palava Sauce

Ingredients:

- 1 lb beef or chicken, cubed
- 1 onion, chopped
- 2 cloves garlic, minced
- 1/2 cup palm oil
- 2 tbsp tomato paste
- 1/4 cup peanut butter
- 2 cups water
- 1 cup spinach or collard greens, chopped
- Salt and pepper to taste

Instructions:

1. Heat palm oil in a pot and sauté onions and garlic.
2. Add meat and brown on all sides.
3. Stir in tomato paste, peanut butter, and water. Simmer for 30 minutes.
4. Add spinach or collard greens and cook for an additional 10 minutes.
5. Season with salt and pepper, then serve with rice.

Nigerian Efo Riro

Ingredients:

- 2 cups spinach, chopped
- 1 lb beef or goat meat, cooked and cubed
- 1 onion, chopped
- 3 tomatoes, blended
- 1/4 cup palm oil
- 2 tbsp ground crayfish
- 2 scotch bonnet peppers, minced
- Salt to taste

Instructions:

1. Heat palm oil in a pan and sauté onions and peppers.
2. Stir in blended tomatoes and cook for 10 minutes.
3. Add the cooked meat and ground crayfish, then simmer for 10 more minutes.
4. Stir in chopped spinach and cook for 5 minutes.
5. Season with salt and serve with rice or fufu.

South African Chakalaka

Ingredients:

- 2 cups mixed vegetables (carrots, beans, peppers)
- 1 onion, chopped
- 1 tbsp curry powder
- 1 tsp paprika
- 2 tomatoes, chopped
- 1 can baked beans, drained
- 1/4 cup vegetable oil
- Salt and pepper to taste

Instructions:

1. Heat oil in a pan and sauté onions, curry powder, and paprika until fragrant.
2. Stir in tomatoes and cook for 10 minutes.
3. Add the mixed vegetables, baked beans, and simmer for another 10 minutes.
4. Season with salt and pepper, and serve as a side dish.

Tunisian Brik

Ingredients:

- 1 package phyllo dough
- 4 eggs
- 1/2 lb tuna, drained
- 1/4 cup parsley, chopped
- 1/4 cup capers
- 1/2 tsp cumin
- Vegetable oil for frying
- Salt and pepper to taste

Instructions:

1. Lay a sheet of phyllo dough and place a spoonful of tuna, parsley, capers, and spices in the center.
2. Crack an egg over the filling.
3. Fold the phyllo dough over to create a triangle, sealing the edges with water.
4. Heat oil in a pan and fry the briks until golden and crispy.
5. Drain on paper towels and serve hot.

Senegalese Thieboudienne

Ingredients:

- 2 lbs white fish (such as tilapia or snapper), cleaned and gutted
- 2 cups long-grain rice
- 2 tablespoons vegetable oil
- 1 onion, chopped
- 2 tomatoes, blended
- 1 tablespoon tomato paste
- 2 carrots, sliced
- 1 eggplant, chopped
- 1/2 head of cabbage, chopped
- 1 sweet pepper, chopped
- 4 cloves garlic, minced
- 2 teaspoons ground cumin
- 1 teaspoon ground coriander
- 1 teaspoon paprika
- Salt and pepper to taste
- Fresh parsley for garnish

Instructions:

1. In a large pot, heat the oil over medium heat. Add onions and garlic, cooking until softened.
2. Add the tomatoes, tomato paste, cumin, coriander, and paprika. Stir and cook for 10 minutes until the sauce thickens.
3. Add the fish to the pot and cook for 10-15 minutes.
4. Add the carrots, eggplant, cabbage, and sweet pepper. Stir and cook for 15-20 minutes until vegetables are tender.
5. Add rice, then pour in water to cover the rice by about an inch. Season with salt and pepper.
6. Cover and cook on low heat for 25-30 minutes, until the rice is fully cooked.
7. Garnish with fresh parsley and serve.

Ugandan Rolex

Ingredients:

- 2 eggs
- 2 chapati (or flatbread)
- 1 onion, chopped
- 1 tomato, chopped
- 1/2 bell pepper, chopped
- 1/2 cup cabbage, shredded
- 2 tablespoons vegetable oil
- Salt and pepper to taste

Instructions:

1. Heat oil in a pan and sauté onions, bell pepper, and tomato until softened.
2. Add cabbage to the pan and stir-fry for 3-4 minutes. Season with salt and pepper.
3. In another pan, cook eggs to your preference (scrambled works best).
4. Lay a chapati flat and spread the vegetable mixture over it.
5. Add the scrambled eggs on top of the veggies and roll the chapati tightly to form a wrap.
6. Serve immediately, wrapped in parchment or foil.

Malawian Nsima with Stew

Ingredients:
For Nsima:

- 2 cups maize flour (cornmeal)
- 4 cups water
- Salt to taste

For Stew:

- 1 lb beef or chicken, cubed
- 1 onion, chopped
- 2 tomatoes, chopped
- 1 bell pepper, chopped
- 2 cloves garlic, minced
- 1 tablespoon vegetable oil
- 1 tablespoon curry powder
- Salt and pepper to taste

Instructions:

1. **To make Nsima:** Bring water to a boil in a pot. Gradually add maize flour while stirring to avoid lumps. Continue stirring until the mixture thickens and becomes smooth. Cook for 5-10 minutes.
2. **To make the stew:** In a large pan, heat oil over medium heat. Add onions and garlic, cooking until soft.
3. Add the meat and brown on all sides. Stir in tomatoes, bell pepper, curry powder, salt, and pepper.
4. Add a little water to the pan and simmer for 20-25 minutes until the meat is tender.
5. Serve the Nsima with the stew on the side.

Moroccan Harira Soup

Ingredients:

- 1 lb lamb or beef, cubed
- 1 onion, chopped
- 2 tomatoes, chopped
- 1 cup lentils, rinsed
- 1/2 cup chickpeas (soaked overnight)
- 1 tablespoon tomato paste
- 1 teaspoon ground ginger
- 1 teaspoon ground cinnamon
- 1 teaspoon turmeric
- 1 teaspoon paprika
- Salt and pepper to taste
- 1/2 cup fresh cilantro, chopped
- 1/4 cup fresh parsley, chopped
- 2 tablespoons lemon juice
- 6 cups water

Instructions:

1. In a large pot, heat oil and sauté the lamb or beef until browned.
2. Add the onion, garlic, and spices. Stir and cook for 5 minutes.
3. Add tomatoes, tomato paste, lentils, chickpeas, and water. Bring to a boil.
4. Reduce heat and simmer for 45 minutes, until the lentils and chickpeas are tender.
5. Stir in the fresh herbs, lemon juice, salt, and pepper. Simmer for another 5 minutes.
6. Serve hot, garnished with extra cilantro and parsley.

Nigerian Ofada Rice with Ayamase

Ingredients:
For Ofada Rice:

- 2 cups Ofada rice (or brown rice as a substitute)
- 4 cups water
- Salt to taste

For Ayamase (Green Pepper Sauce):

- 6 green bell peppers
- 2 scotch bonnet peppers
- 1 onion, chopped
- 1/4 cup palm oil
- 2 cloves garlic, minced
- 1 teaspoon ground crayfish
- 1/2 lb beef or goat meat, cubed
- 2 tablespoons tomato paste
- Salt and pepper to taste

Instructions:

1. **For the rice:** Wash the Ofada rice thoroughly. Bring water to a boil in a pot and add the rice. Cook for 25-30 minutes, until tender.
2. **For the Ayamase sauce:** Blend the green bell peppers, scotch bonnet peppers, and onions into a smooth paste.
3. Heat palm oil in a pan over medium heat. Add the garlic and cook until fragrant.
4. Stir in the blended pepper paste and cook for 10 minutes until the oil separates.
5. Add the meat, tomato paste, crayfish, salt, and pepper. Cook for another 10-15 minutes until the meat is tender.
6. Serve the Ayamase sauce over the Ofada rice.

Kenyan Samosa

Ingredients:

- 1 lb ground beef or chicken
- 1 onion, chopped
- 2 cloves garlic, minced
- 1 tablespoon ground cumin
- 1 teaspoon ground coriander
- 1/2 teaspoon ground turmeric
- 1/4 teaspoon ground cinnamon
- 1/2 cup peas
- 1 package of samosa wrappers or phyllo dough
- Vegetable oil for frying
- Salt and pepper to taste

Instructions:

1. Heat oil in a pan and sauté onions and garlic until soft.
2. Add ground meat and cook until browned.
3. Stir in the cumin, coriander, turmeric, cinnamon, and peas. Cook for 5-7 minutes until the peas are tender.
4. Allow the mixture to cool.
5. Place a spoonful of the filling into each samosa wrapper, fold into a triangle, and seal with a little water.
6. Heat oil in a pan and fry the samosas until golden brown and crispy.
7. Drain on paper towels and serve with a dipping sauce.

West African Groundnut Stew

Ingredients:

- 1 lb chicken (or beef), cubed
- 1 onion, chopped
- 2 cloves garlic, minced
- 1 tablespoon grated ginger
- 2 tomatoes, chopped
- 1/4 cup peanut butter (or ground peanuts)
- 4 cups chicken or vegetable broth
- 1 teaspoon ground cumin
- 1 teaspoon paprika
- 1/2 teaspoon cayenne pepper (optional)
- Salt and pepper to taste
- 1/2 cup chopped spinach or kale
- 2 tablespoons vegetable oil

Instructions:

1. Heat oil in a large pot over medium heat. Add the chicken and cook until browned on all sides. Remove and set aside.
2. In the same pot, sauté onions, garlic, and ginger until soft.
3. Add tomatoes, cumin, paprika, and cayenne pepper. Stir and cook for 5-7 minutes until the tomatoes break down.
4. Stir in peanut butter, then slowly add the broth, mixing until the peanut butter is well incorporated.
5. Return the chicken to the pot and bring the mixture to a simmer. Cook for 20-25 minutes.
6. Add the spinach or kale, and cook for an additional 5 minutes.
7. Season with salt and pepper, and serve hot with rice or flatbread.

Sudanese Ful Medames

Ingredients:

- 2 cups dried fava beans, soaked overnight
- 1 onion, chopped
- 2 cloves garlic, minced
- 1 tablespoon ground cumin
- 1 tablespoon ground coriander
- 1 tablespoon lemon juice
- 2 tablespoons olive oil
- Salt and pepper to taste
- Chopped parsley for garnish
- 2 hard-boiled eggs, chopped (optional)

Instructions:

1. Drain and rinse the soaked fava beans. Place them in a large pot with water and bring to a boil. Lower the heat and simmer for 45-60 minutes, or until tender.
2. In a separate pan, heat olive oil over medium heat. Sauté onions and garlic until soft.
3. Add the cumin and coriander to the onions and cook for 1-2 minutes until fragrant.
4. Add the cooked fava beans to the pan, stirring gently. Pour in the lemon juice and season with salt and pepper.
5. Mash the beans slightly for a creamy consistency.
6. Serve topped with chopped parsley and hard-boiled eggs, if desired. Enjoy with warm flatbread.

Somali Camel Stew

Ingredients:

- 1 lb camel meat (or beef), cubed
- 1 onion, chopped
- 2 cloves garlic, minced
- 1 tablespoon grated ginger
- 2 tomatoes, chopped
- 1 teaspoon ground cinnamon
- 1 teaspoon ground cumin
- 1 teaspoon turmeric
- 1/2 teaspoon black pepper
- 1 tablespoon tomato paste
- 2 cups beef or lamb broth
- 2 tablespoons vegetable oil
- Salt to taste
- Fresh cilantro for garnish

Instructions:

1. Heat oil in a large pot over medium heat. Brown the camel meat on all sides. Remove and set aside.
2. In the same pot, sauté onions, garlic, and ginger until softened.
3. Add the tomatoes, cinnamon, cumin, turmeric, black pepper, and tomato paste. Cook for 5 minutes until fragrant.
4. Return the meat to the pot, then add the broth. Bring to a simmer, cover, and cook for 1-1.5 hours, until the meat is tender.
5. Season with salt to taste.
6. Garnish with fresh cilantro and serve with rice or flatbread.

Namibian Potjie

Ingredients:

- 2 lbs beef or game meat, cubed
- 1 onion, chopped
- 2 carrots, sliced
- 2 potatoes, peeled and cubed
- 2 tomatoes, chopped
- 1 tablespoon tomato paste
- 1/2 cup red wine (optional)
- 2 cups beef broth
- 1 tablespoon ground coriander
- 1 tablespoon paprika
- 1 teaspoon thyme
- 2 cloves garlic, minced
- Salt and pepper to taste
- Fresh parsley for garnish

Instructions:

1. Heat a potjie or heavy pot over medium heat and brown the meat in batches. Remove and set aside.
2. In the same pot, sauté onions, garlic, carrots, and potatoes until softened.
3. Stir in the tomatoes, tomato paste, ground coriander, paprika, and thyme.
4. Add the meat back to the pot along with the red wine (if using) and beef broth. Stir and bring to a simmer.
5. Cover and cook on low heat for 2-3 hours, stirring occasionally, until the meat is tender and the flavors have melded together.
6. Season with salt and pepper to taste, and garnish with fresh parsley.
7. Serve hot with rice or bread.

Tanzanian Sukuma with Eggs

Ingredients:

- 1 bunch sukuma (collard greens or kale), chopped
- 2 tablespoons vegetable oil
- 1 onion, chopped
- 2 tomatoes, chopped
- 2 cloves garlic, minced
- 1/2 teaspoon ground cumin
- 1/2 teaspoon turmeric
- Salt and pepper to taste
- 4 eggs
- Water as needed

Instructions:

1. Heat oil in a large pan over medium heat. Add onions and garlic, sautéing until soft.
2. Add tomatoes, cumin, turmeric, salt, and pepper. Cook for 5 minutes until the tomatoes break down.
3. Stir in the chopped sukuma and add a small amount of water (just enough to cover the vegetables). Cook for 10-15 minutes, until the greens are tender.
4. In a separate pan, fry the eggs to your preference (fried or scrambled).
5. Serve the sukuma alongside the fried eggs.

Ivory Coast Attiéké with Fish

Ingredients:

- 2 cups attiéké (cassava couscous)
- 1 lb white fish (tilapia or snapper), fried
- 1 onion, chopped
- 2 tomatoes, chopped
- 1/2 cup vegetable broth
- 1 tablespoon vegetable oil
- 2 cloves garlic, minced
- 1 teaspoon ground ginger
- 1 teaspoon paprika
- Salt and pepper to taste
- Fresh cilantro for garnish

Instructions:

1. Prepare the attiéké according to the package instructions, steaming it until fluffy.
2. In a pan, heat oil and sauté onions and garlic until soft.
3. Add the tomatoes, ginger, paprika, salt, and pepper, cooking for 5-7 minutes.
4. Pour in the vegetable broth and cook for another 10 minutes until the sauce thickens.
5. Serve the fried fish on top of the attiéké and spoon the sauce over the top.
6. Garnish with fresh cilantro and serve hot.